ANNE HARDY

Survival Spell

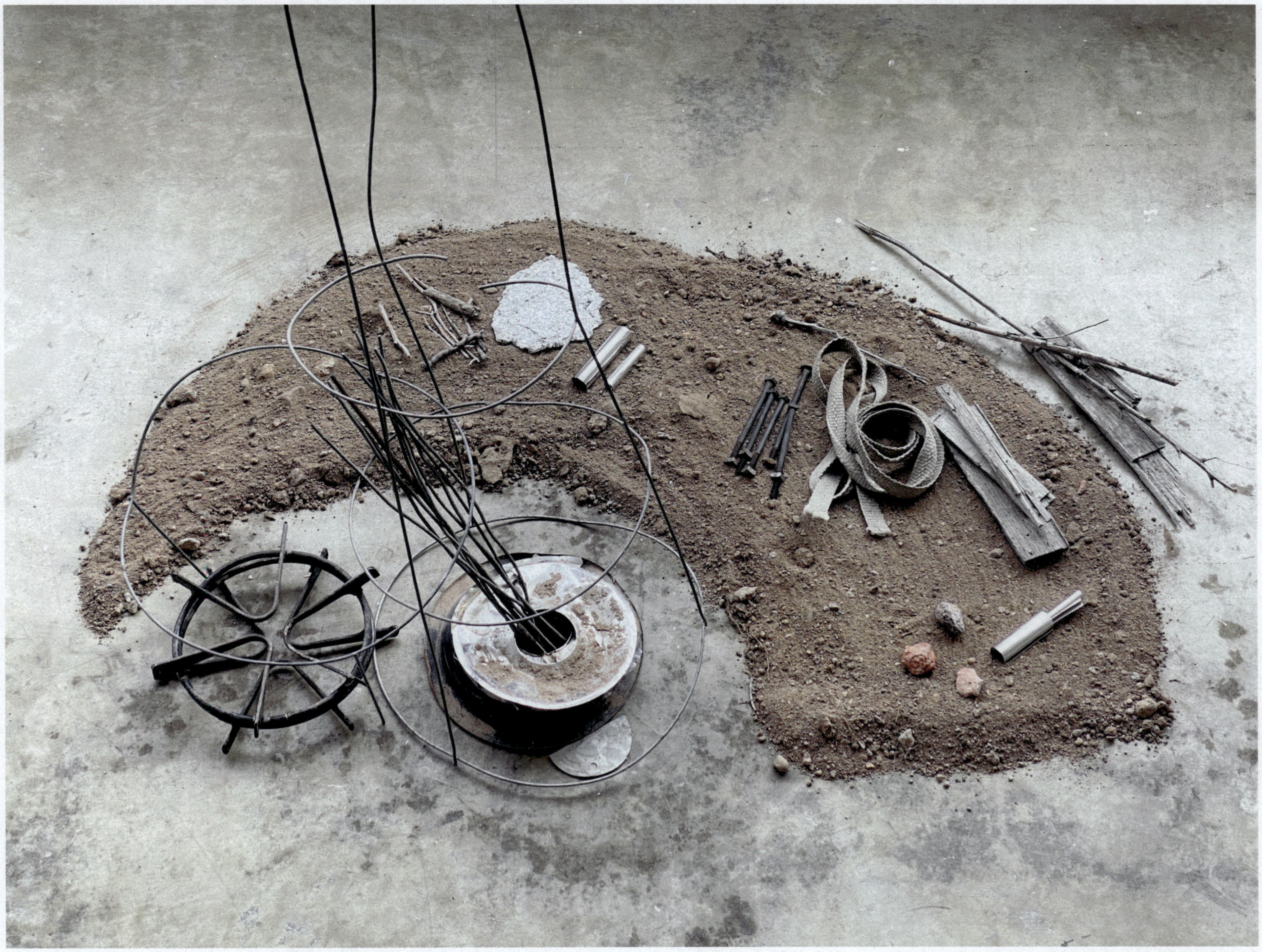

Survival Spell, **Anne Hardy**

This book was published on the occasion of the exhibition Anne Hardy *Survival Spell* at Maureen Paley and Studio M, London 6 April—19 May 2024.

Published by Maureen Paley, London and Dent—De—Leone, 2024

Images 2024 © Anne Hardy, courtesy Maureen Paley, London. Text © Lisa Le Feuvre

Designed by Kajsa of Åbäke
Printed by newspaperclub.com

MAUREEN PALEY
60 Three Colts Lane
London E2 6GQ
maureenpaley.com

Dent—De—Leone,
48 Wilton Way,
E8 1BG London, UK
dentdeleone.com

ISBN 978—1—907908—87—3

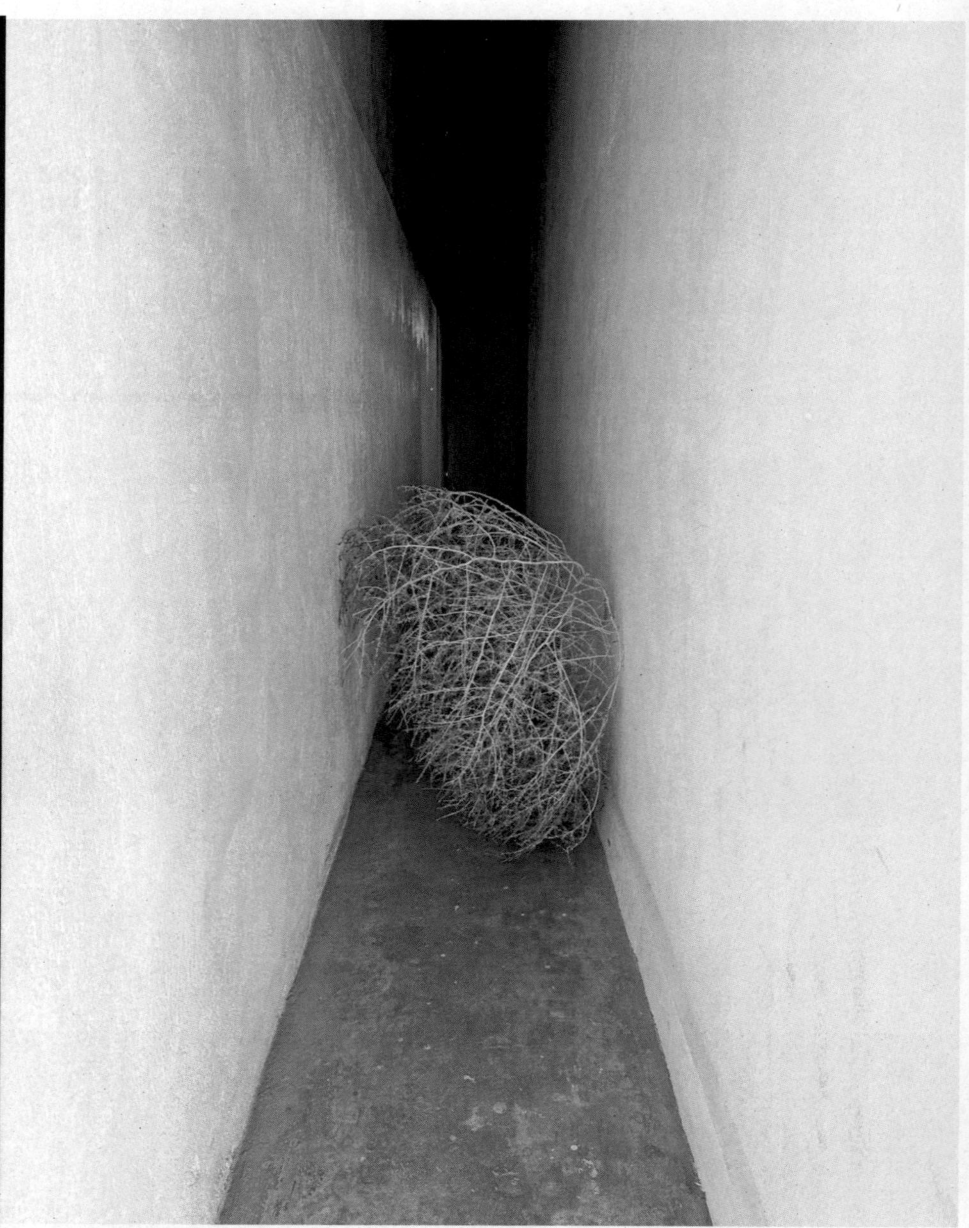

2. *Unexpected Obstacle,* **2022**
Tumbleweed, corridor
dimensions variable

Cover:
Survival Spell, **2022—24**
Found materials, earth, cast pewter, Chinati rocks
H 85 x W 115 x L 75 cm

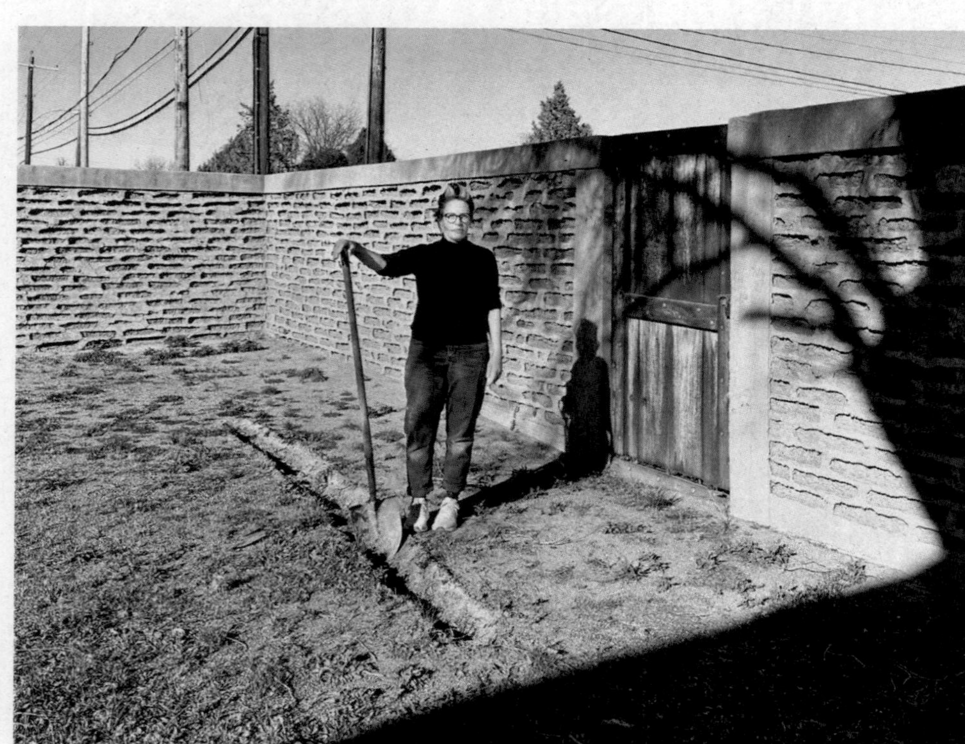

1. Anne Hardy, Chinati Foundation, Marfa, Texas, USA, **2022**

Image Credits:

Cover, 1, 2, 4, 5, 6, 7, 8, 9, 17, 18, 20, 21 installation views
The Locker Plant, Chinati Foundation, Marfa.

10, 11, 12, 13, 14, 15, 16 installation views Maureen Paley and Studio M, London.

Photography Anne Hardy / Angus Mill **3, 19, 22, 23** installation views, studio, London. Photography Anne Hardy / Angus Mill

All photographs ©Anne Hardy
Photography Anne Hardy/Angus Mill

Thank you:

Angus Mill, Maureen Paley, Kajsa Ståhl, Lisa Le Feuvre, Paulina Lenoir, Sebastian Thomas, Robert Prouse, The Chinati Foundation, Ingrid Schaffner, Chris Taylor, Steven Martin, Karina Salcido, Rob Weiner, Yutaka Kikutake, Tomoya Matsuzaki, Nahoko Matsuzaki, Lauren Williamson, Oliver Evans, Mike Iveson, Naja Bak Rantorp, Rie Marsden, Jonathon Cresswell, Madeleine Pledge, Milo McKinnon, Kate Kadeniuk.

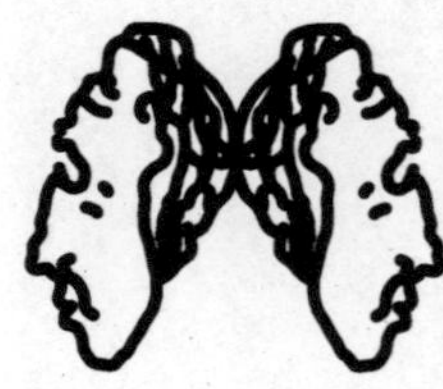

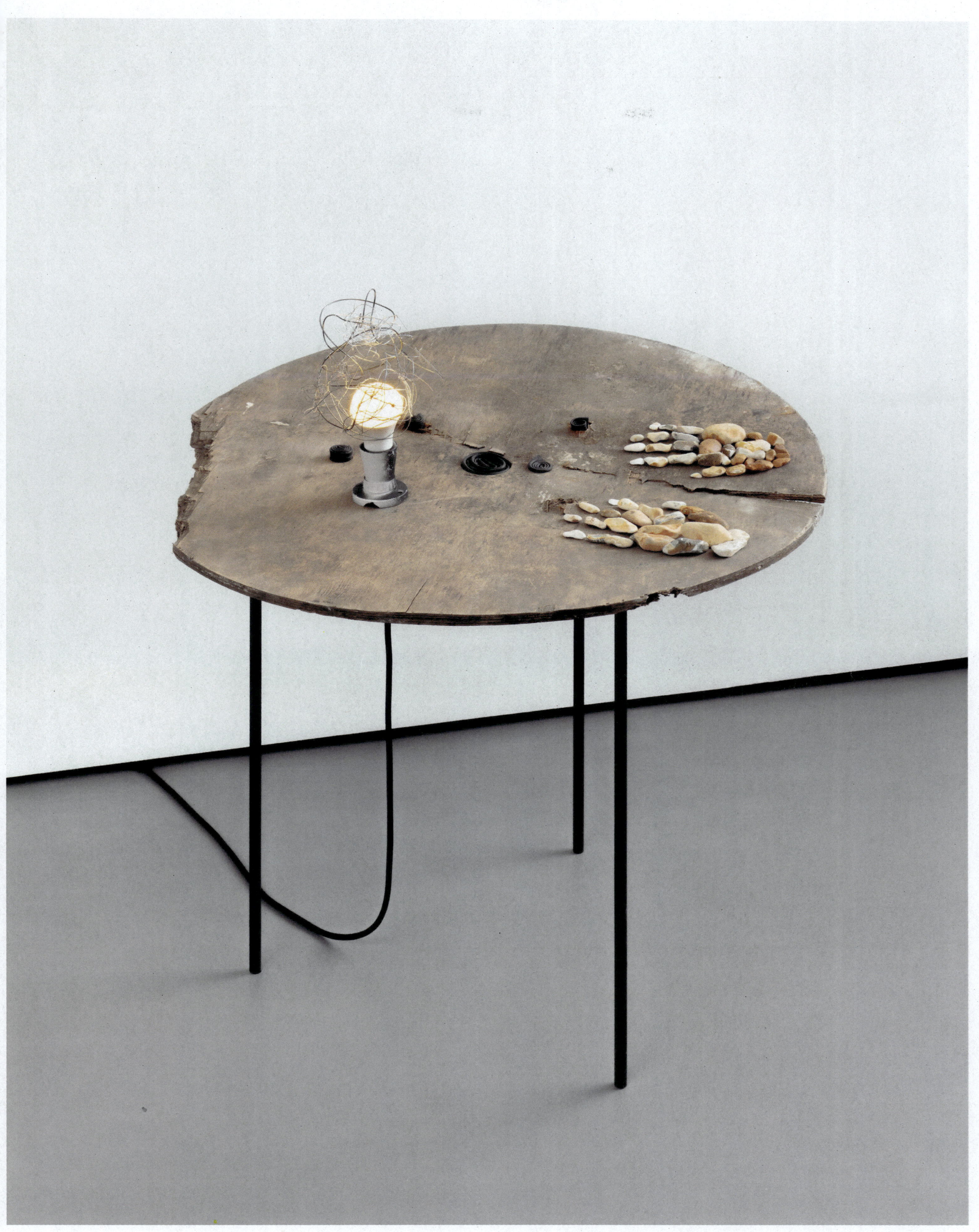

3. *Energy Locator,* **2023–24**
**Found materials, stones, welded steel, light,
custom-designed computer system for light source
that responds to Marfa meteorological data
H 99 x Ø 81cm**

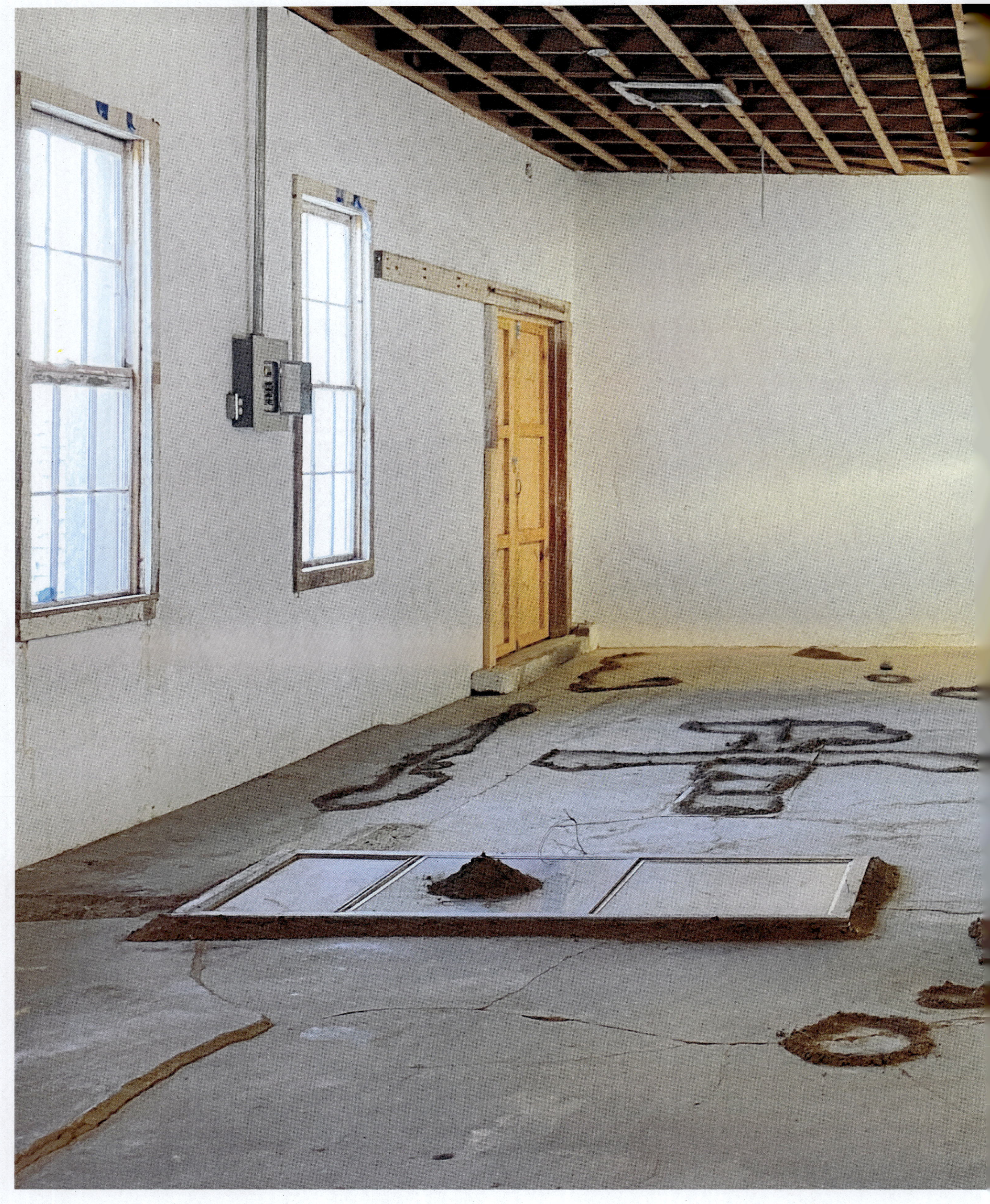

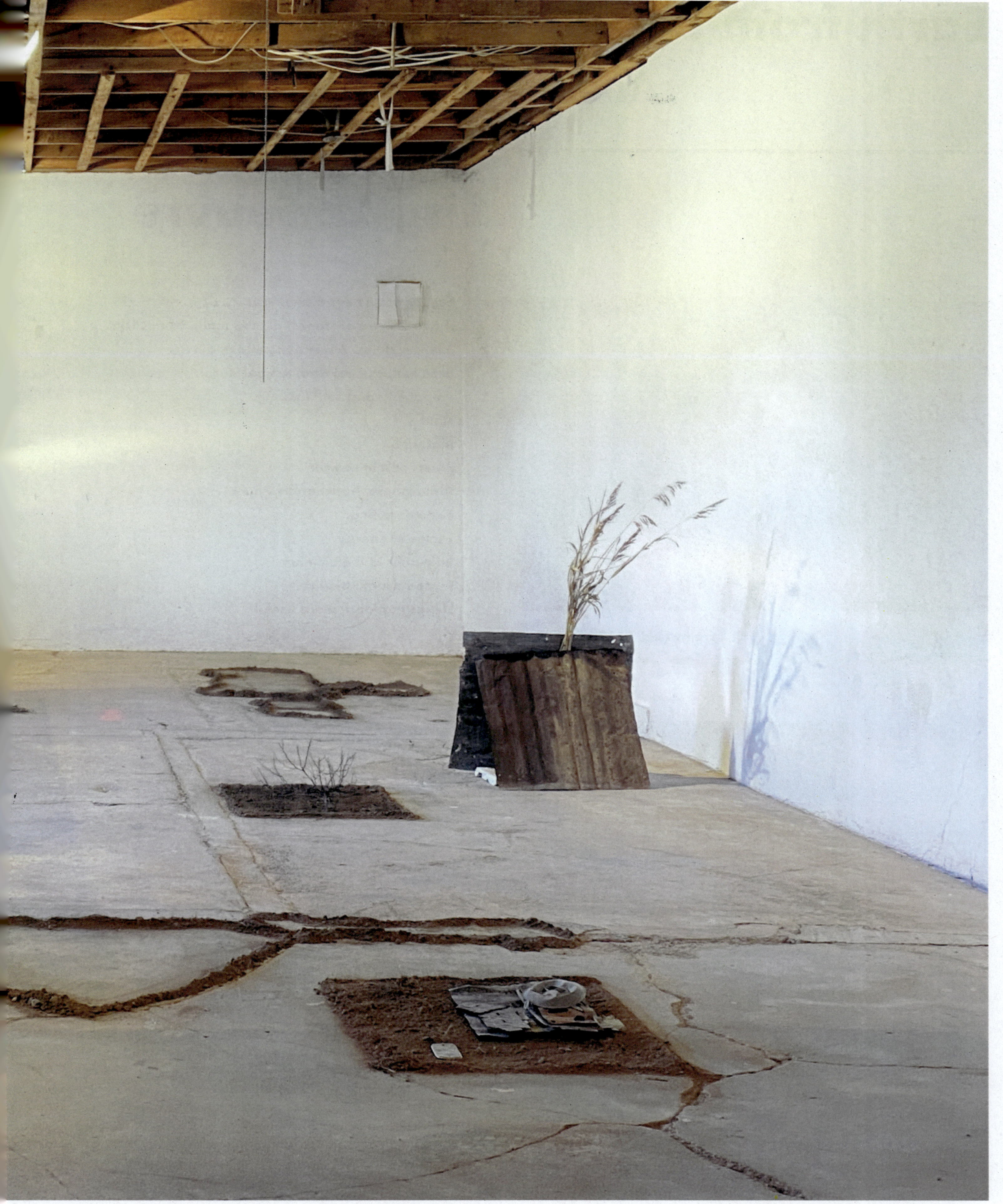

4. *Energy Field*, **2022**
Found materials, Marfa earth, Chinati grass
dimensions variable

Earth from a near elsewhere:
Anne Hardy's spells

Lisa Le Feuvre

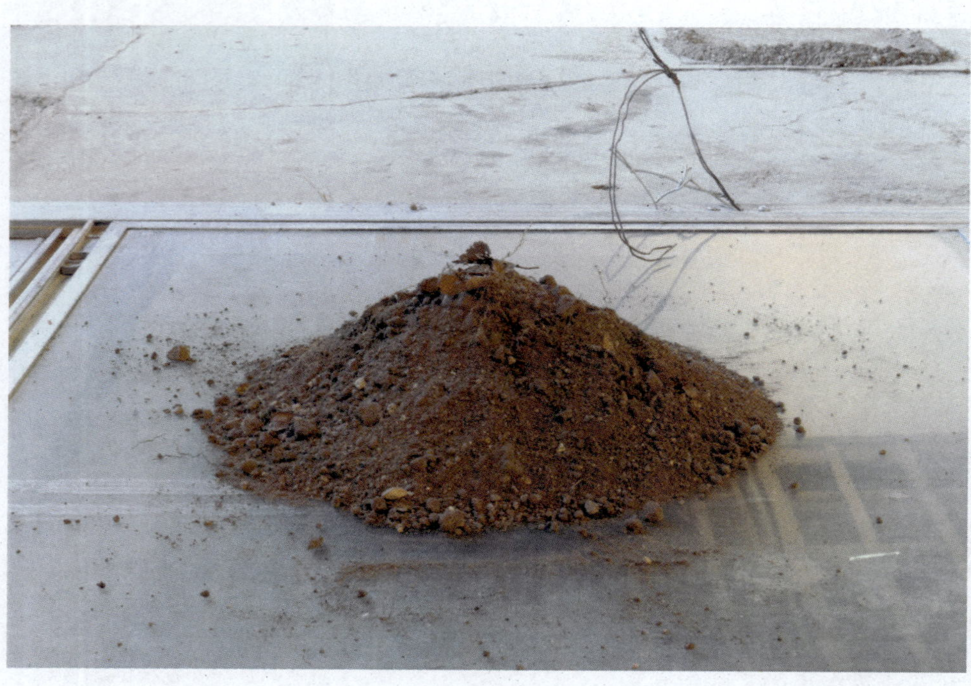

5. *Energy Field,* **2022 (detail)**

Earth from a near elsewhere.
A hand made of stones; a hand made from sticks.
Silence, stains. A micro-mountain, air.
Breezeblocks, texture, temperature.
Palpability and tactility.
Time.
Material.
Beans cast in pewter.
Atmosphere, horizontality, light.
Bodies waiting.
Torsos of energy.
Ring-pulls and aluminium.
Rusted spaghetti wire.
Things that once were useful.

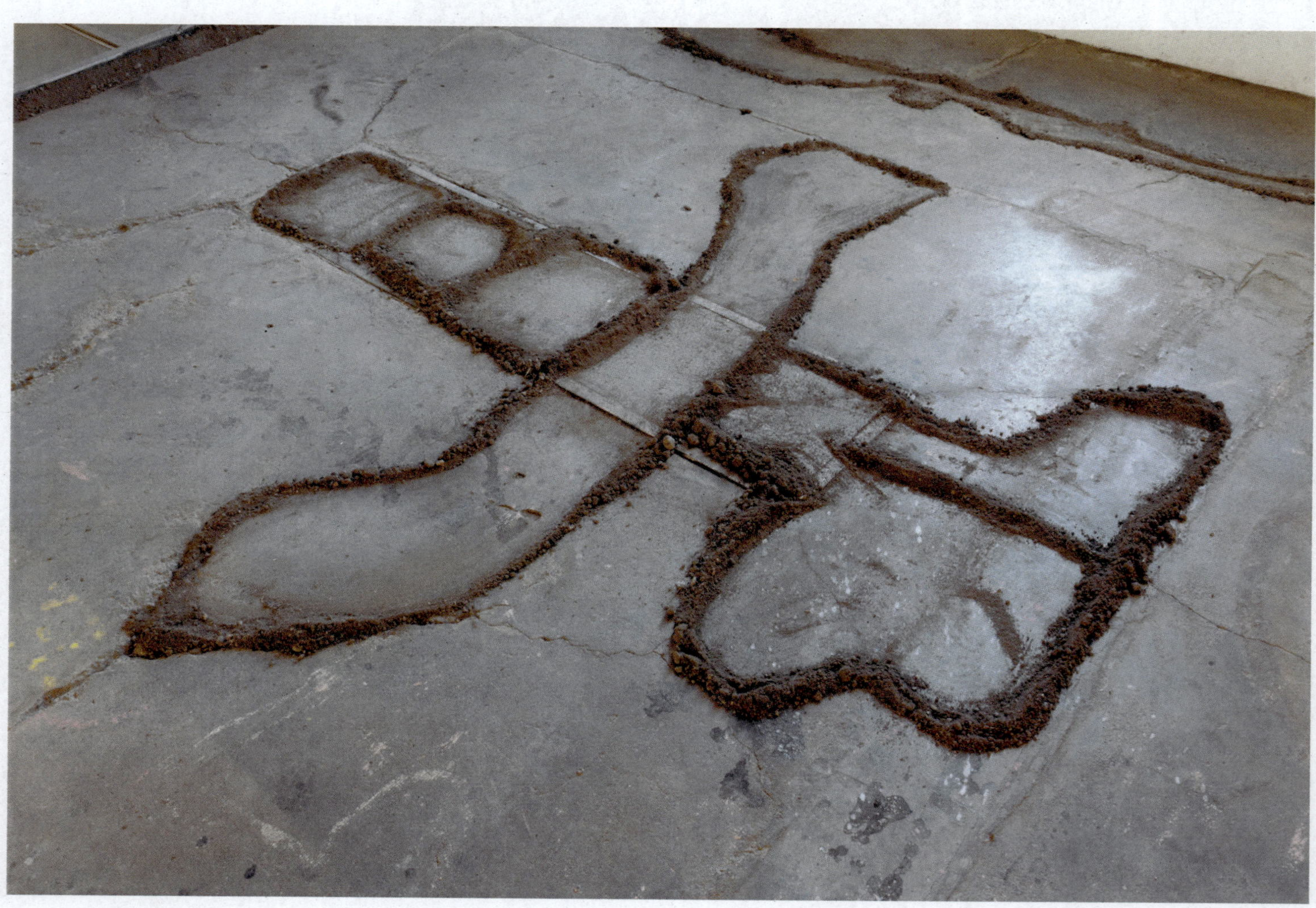

6. *Energy Field,* **2022 (detail)**

Everywhere there is so much stuff, so much material. Human beings make objects to try and make sense of the world around us, to try to make this complicated existence more manageable, to try to take time from time. A folding chair: it takes the load off the legs and is easy to carry and slip away when not needed. Window screens: they let air in and keep bugs out. Light bulbs: allow us to see in the dark. A table: brings the ground to the hand. The objects around us perform magic, they change situations, open possibilities and, sometimes, cause problems. Objects lurk, and they catch the body when its mind is not paying attention, leaving dents and bruises on the skin. And just like those bodies they have been made to serve, these objects age, rip, warp, hold the traces of time, and become invisible. Some objects are dismissed, not seen, taken for granted, and judged as being immaterial to useful life.

But who, and what are invisible? What are the ethics at play? Art gives us moments where we must stop, think, and perceive the systems that pass the value judgements that grease the machines of survival. Language is a system. It's a fallible system, and we often don't notice it until it stops working—when we're trying to find a word or we're trying to say something that exceeds what we are capable of saying. We can't match our feelings. We can't match our ambitions in language. These inherent failures demand that we are circuitous in order to communicate. It's the assumptions that get in the way. It's the stuff in between the words that can be the most invigorating, and the most dangerous, the most harmful. Language creates a system of relationships. Once a belief or a position is placed within a language, that moment of articulation creates relativity. It could be relationships among colours, as in red, green, blue. It could be a relationship to weight or length. It could be materials, both tangible and intangible. These relationships, these relativities, form currency: currency is exchanged, it is the electricity coursing through the power grid, a flow, a movement, presentness.

Anne Hardy gathers leftovers sourced from the peripheries—from the edges of capitalism—into sculptural cosmologies. Each is in a fragile balance, one that holds itself in the present tense. What makes the present visible is the invisibility of the future, the impossibility of seeing what comes next. Hardy's sculptures show how the world is put together, and they are invitations to stop, to look, to look again. This is an exhibition of survival spells, of alchemical accumulations where the mind and body meet. What might be the difference between a spell and a curse? Curses and spells have magical, alchemical, and transformative consequences. They connect the known and the unknown, bringing together what can and what can't be verified with the senses. A curse is an unwanted burden, pushed with maleficence, and out of the control of the one who receives it. A spell is different: it is empowering, it transforms circumstances, conjures results, brings balance through articulation. Curses support systems, but spells reroute and infiltrate them. Every single one of us is a site of values, systems, and assumptions that are both inhabited and projected on to us. We are like sponges, soaking up values and systems. But we are also energy fields, pushing out and pushing against those combinatory and contradictory values and systems. All systems, all values are consensual hallucinations: they must be believed for them to circulate, and at their edges lie very particular sets of relations.

There are figures here among Hardy's spells - two seated bodies waiting, thinking, with open hands. Both have feet shod in elegant boots designed for striding the city. One sits on a box with feet planted in earth and a torso formed of a swirling mass of energy weighted with a building block, beside its hips sit four pewter-cast beans in a paw-like pattern shining silver. Pewter is an alloy, a human-made material that is malleable, making it ideal for working into utilitarian objects, and believed to conduct the perfect energy to amplify spells. This seated figure is named *Being*

(Immaterial); its companion is a kneeling figure identified as *Being (Interloper)*. An interloper is a being in a place where they are not wanted, defined by a system as not belonging. This one's hands are open, and from their shoulders a long tail stretches, at the tip rooting into the earth. One can choose to be an interloper, and one can have that status forced in from the outside: choice and designation are very different sets of operations.

Energy Locator is a warped and perfunctory table – its legs are bendy, and its top is perhaps made from a salvaged industrial cable reel. There are water-warps, cracks, and holes that have been filled with what might be bicycle tyre inner tubes. It supports a pair of hands made from stones that promise a potential of touching, a spell of manual thinking where rocks become as sentient as flesh. These hands are firmly pressing down, as if they are supporting a leaning, heavy body so it can look carefully at a lightbulb that sits on the surface, its power cable stretching out like a tail into a plug socket. This light source fluctuates in response to weather data that is being channelled through the invisible surrounding data networks. Weather is a phenomenon – it is captured in empirical data and is felt subjectively. Once discussing the weather was a banality to pass time and connect with others; now it is a political and urgent matter. Switching on a light in a room opens a connection to power grids, and to the natural resources that have been exploited for our use. Light and language are expansive qualities; finding their limits makes their presence perceivable.

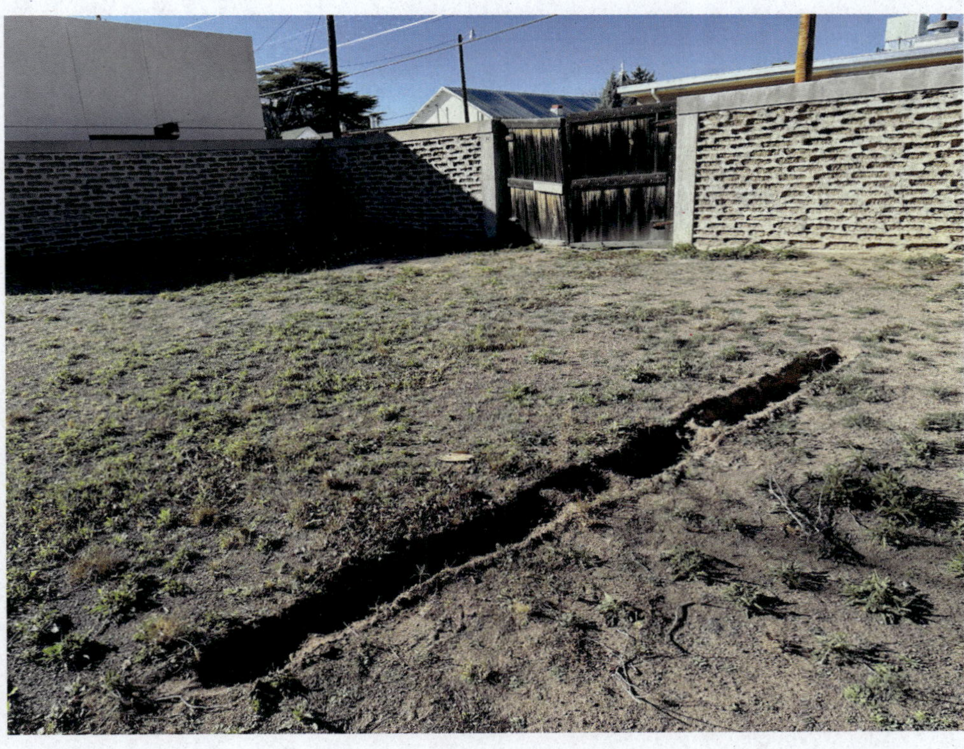

7. *Earth Line*, **2022**
Marfa earth
dimensions variable

Hardy's spells are made from the bare essentials, they are landscapes where the mind and the world meet. *Survival Spell*, the eponymous earthwork, is a curve of dirt on the floor, a gestural sweep that holds within and without its earthy-boundaries once-purposeful fragments. It sits awaiting disturbance, a clumsy foot would undo everything. Somehow it creates a field of energy that pushes back its observers with tenderness. *Survival Spell* was made during the artist's 2022 residency at the Chinati Foundation in Marfa, Texas – a place where the light and horizon feel limitless, a one-crossroads town at the edges of the United States and the desert. It is an edge place with its own edges. Hardy swept earth, dug dirt from the backyard, recorded the sound of snow melting off the roof of the building where she slept, and gathered unwanted objects from the dump. These relics she combs into precise arrangements that vibrate beyond their material form – they are magic, they defy words, and they transform.

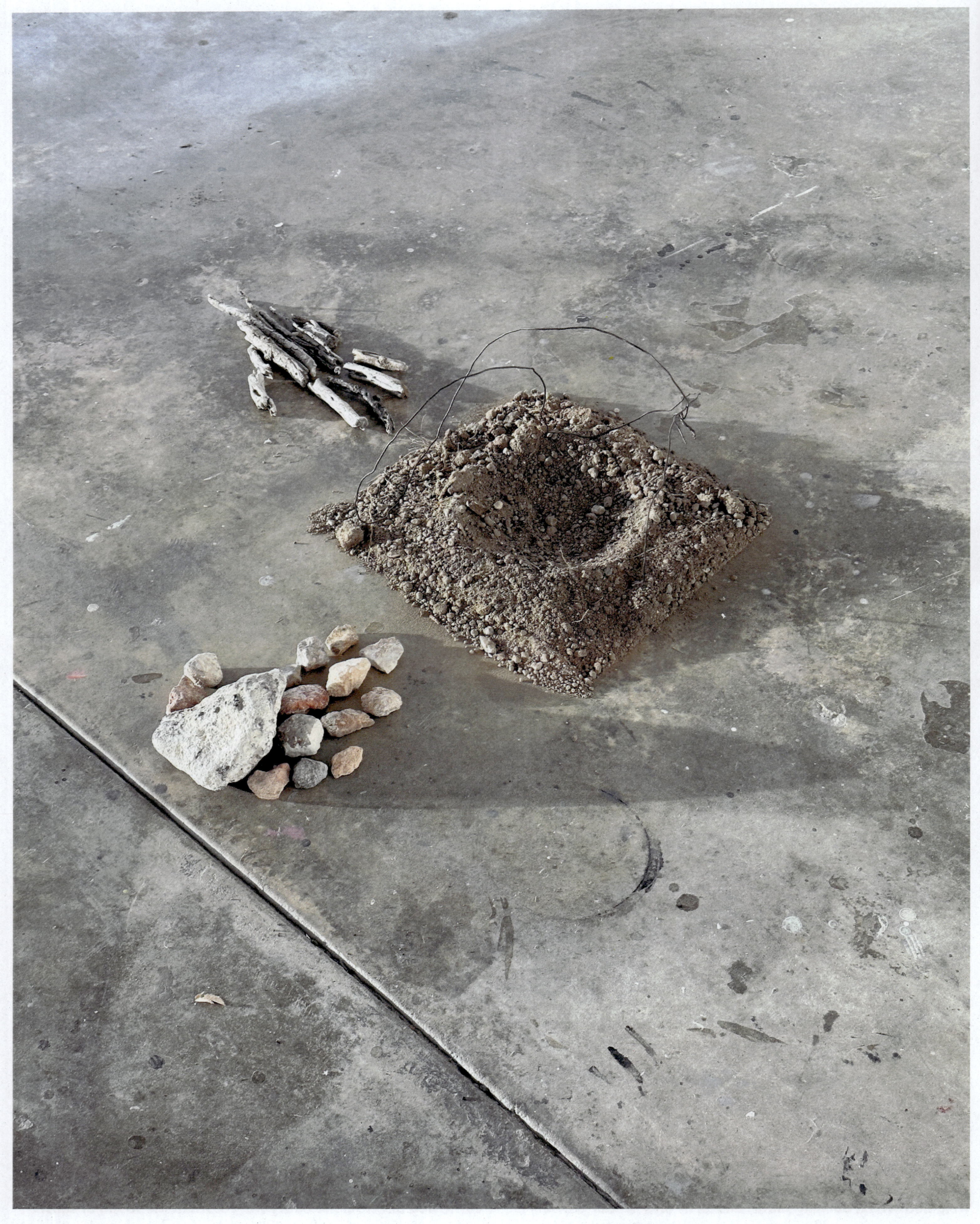

8. *Lure (Incantation)*, **2022–24**
Chinati rocks, sticks, found wire and earth
H 24 x W 62.5 x L 65.5 cm

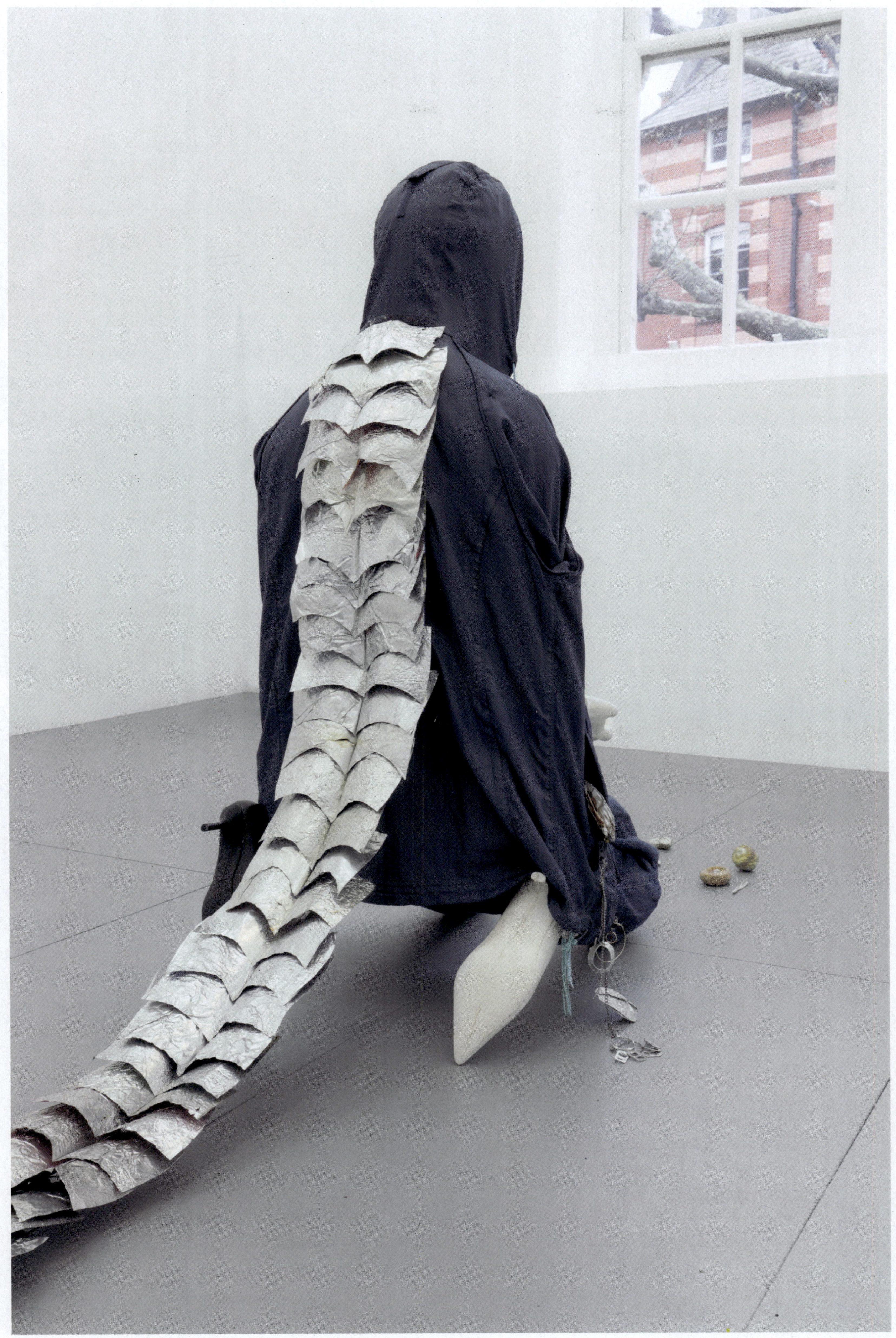

11. *Being (Interloper),* **2022–2024 (detail)**

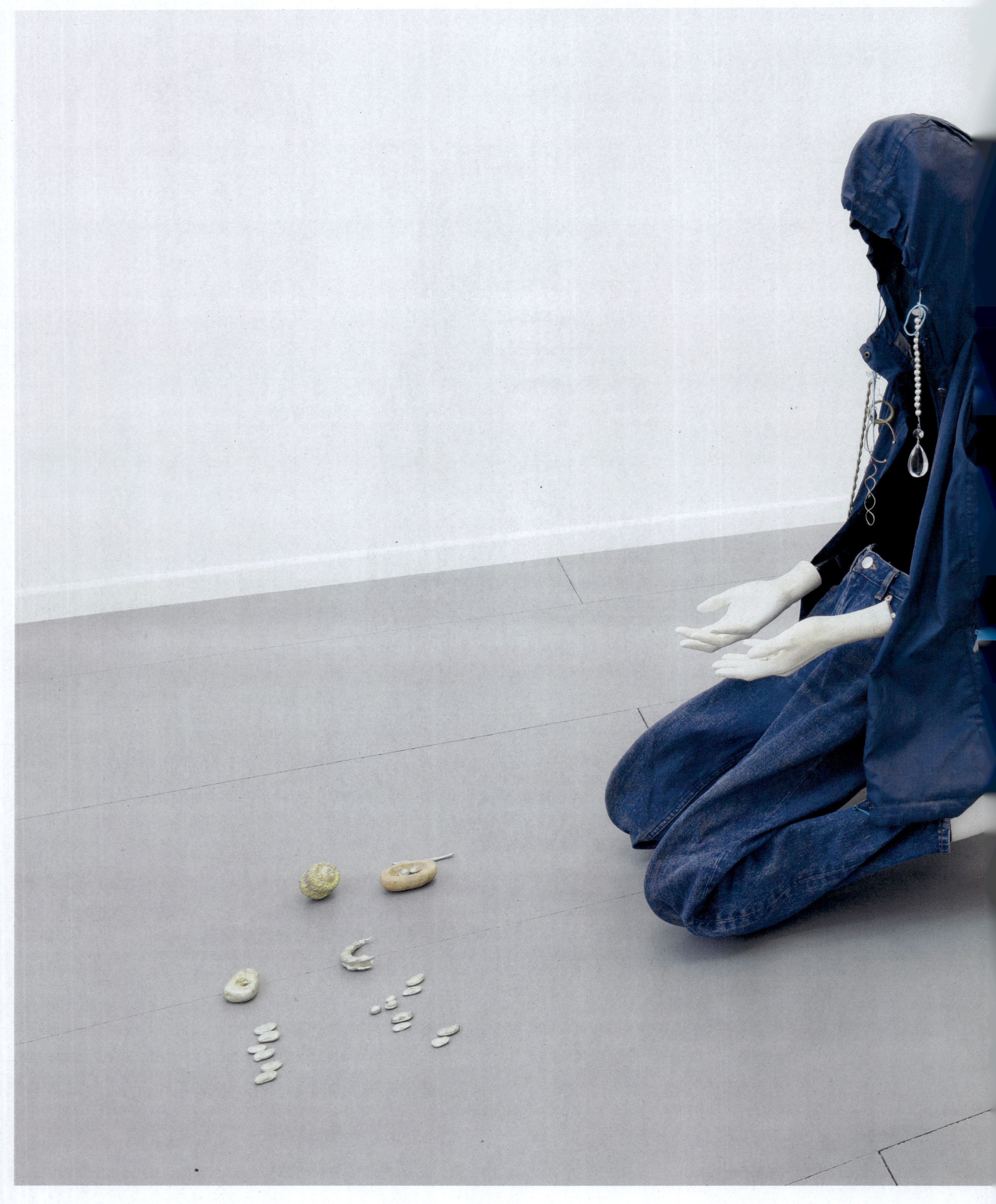

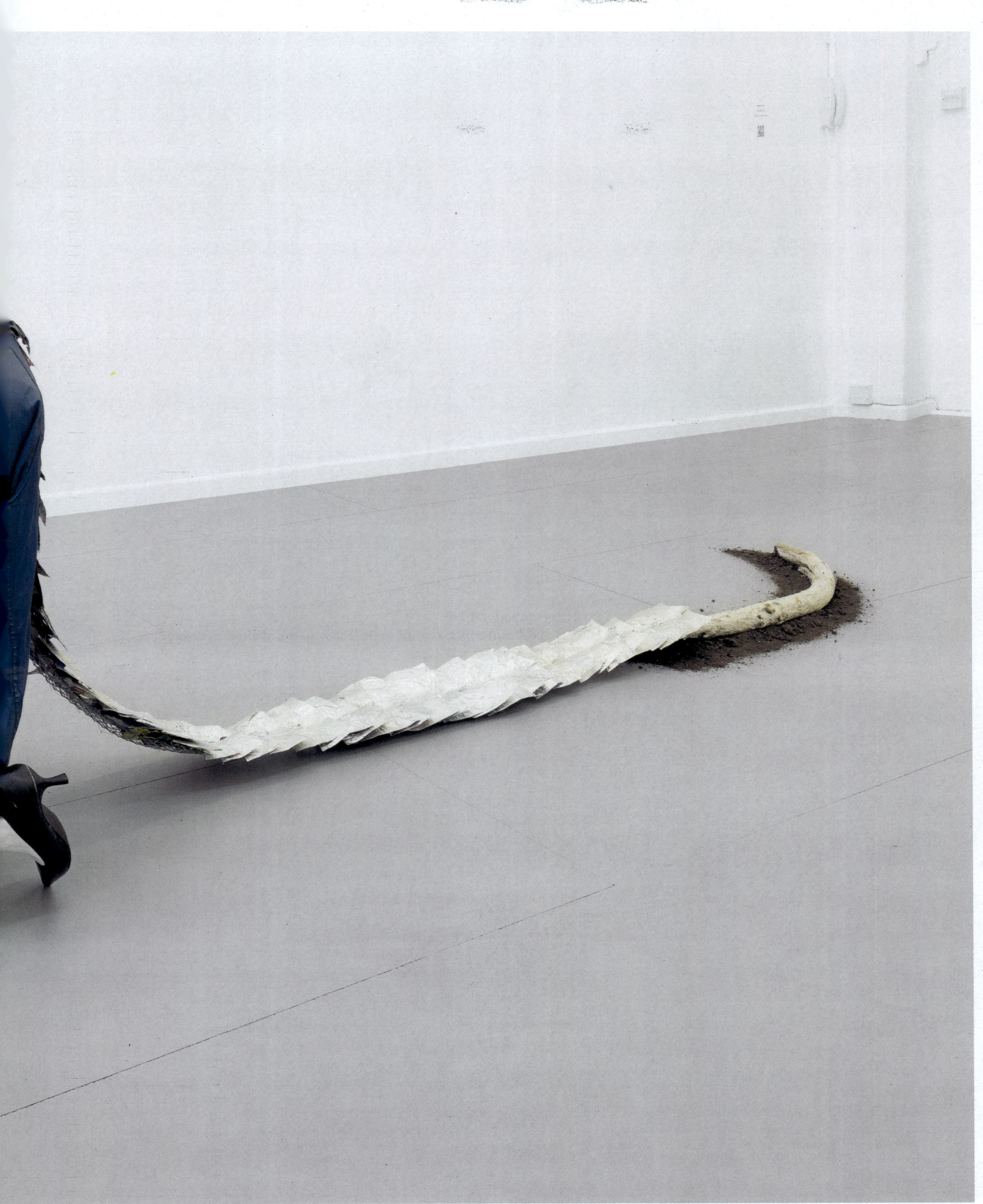

12. *Being (Interloper),* **2022–2024**
**Artists clothes, tin cans crushed by trucks outside the studio, welded steel,
cast pewter, cast jesmonite, jewellery, earth, wood, wire
H 115 x W 55 x L 360 cm**

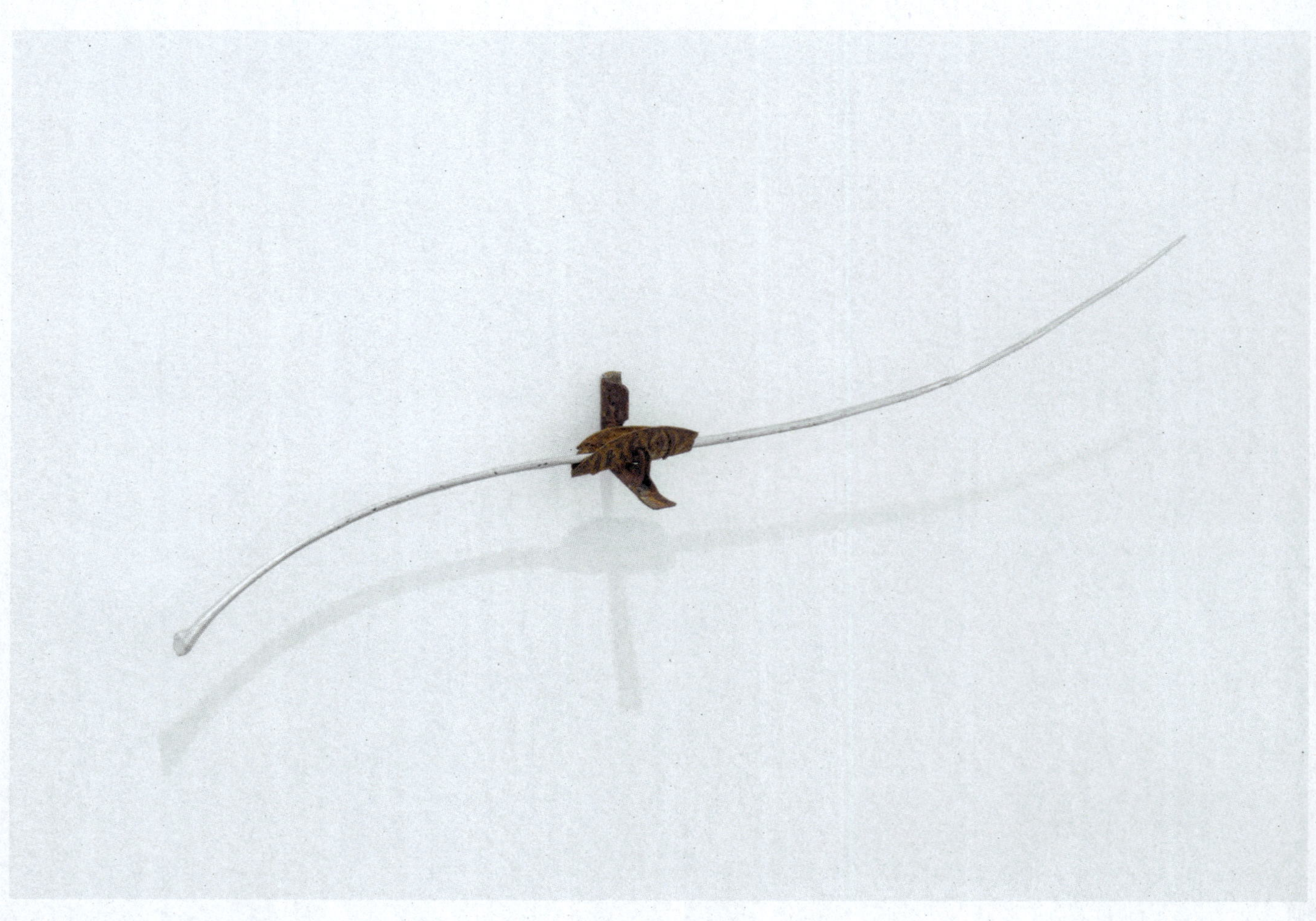

13. *Lure (wand)*, **2024**
Found materials, rusted metal, cast and polished pewter
H 15 x W 70 x D 15 cm

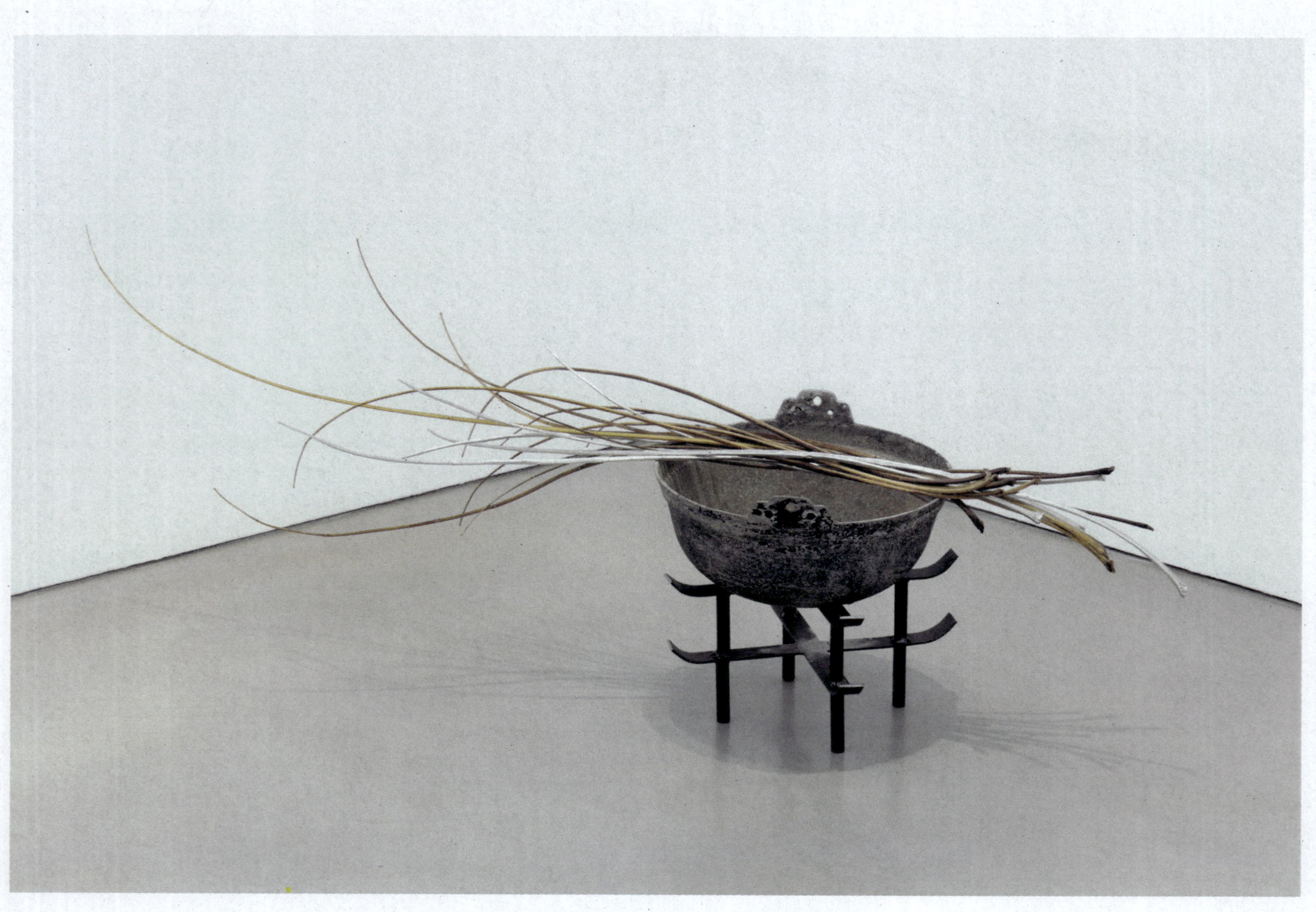

14. *Portal (Fallen Branches)*, **2023–2024**
Found materials, welded steel, cast and polished pewter,
fallen tree branches
H 40 x W 120 x Ø 33 cm

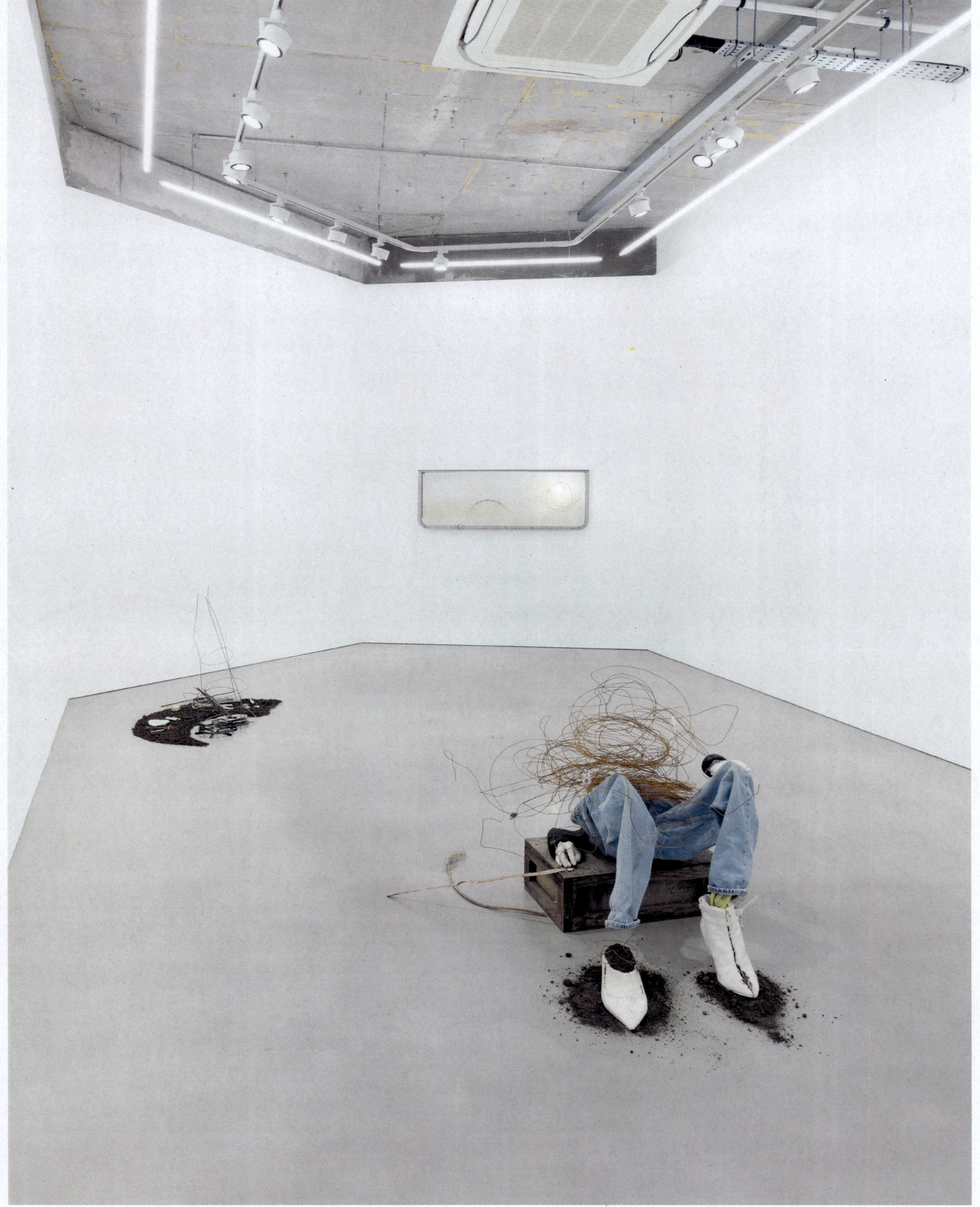

15. *Survival Spell*, **2024 (installation view, Maureen Paley)**

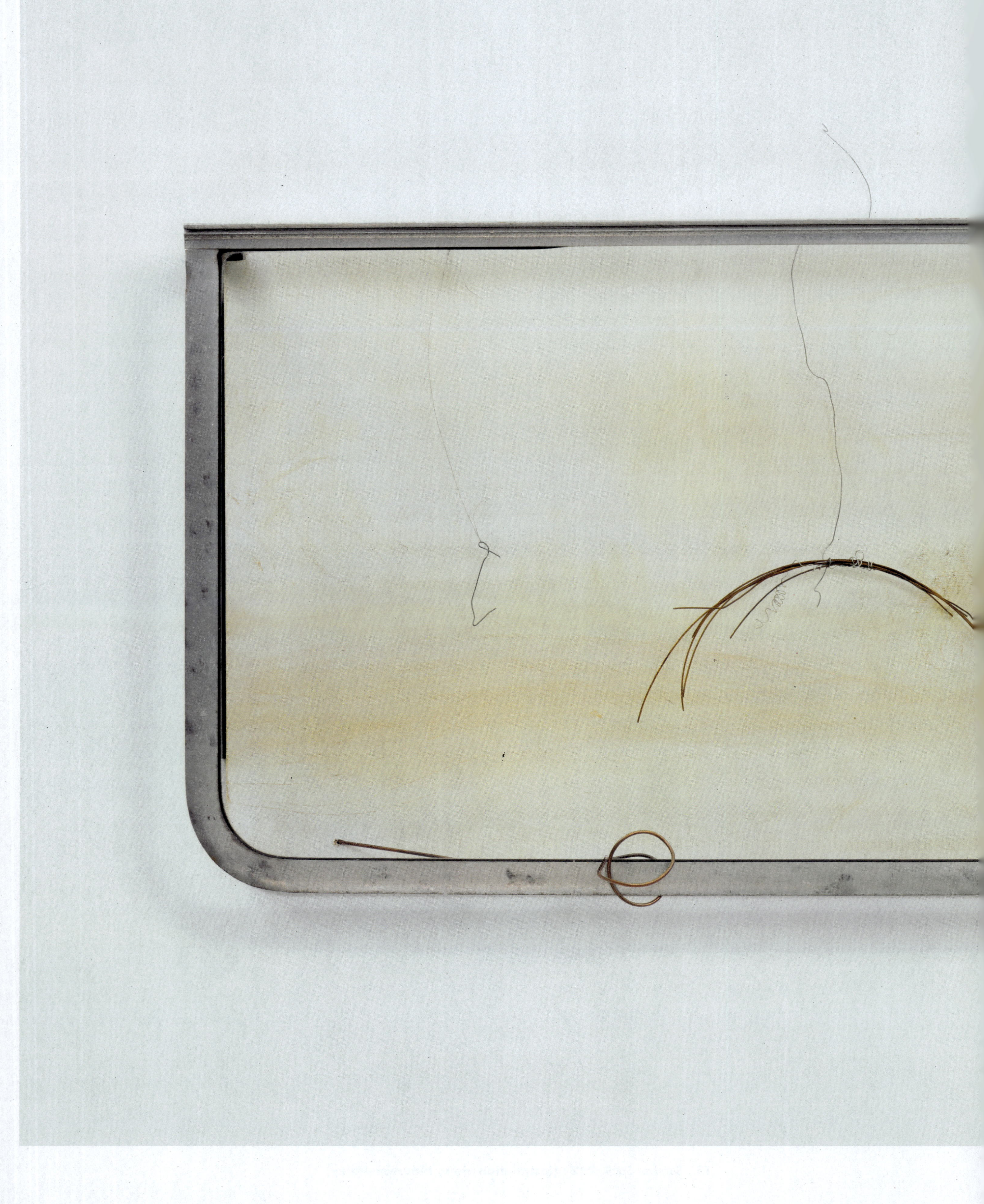

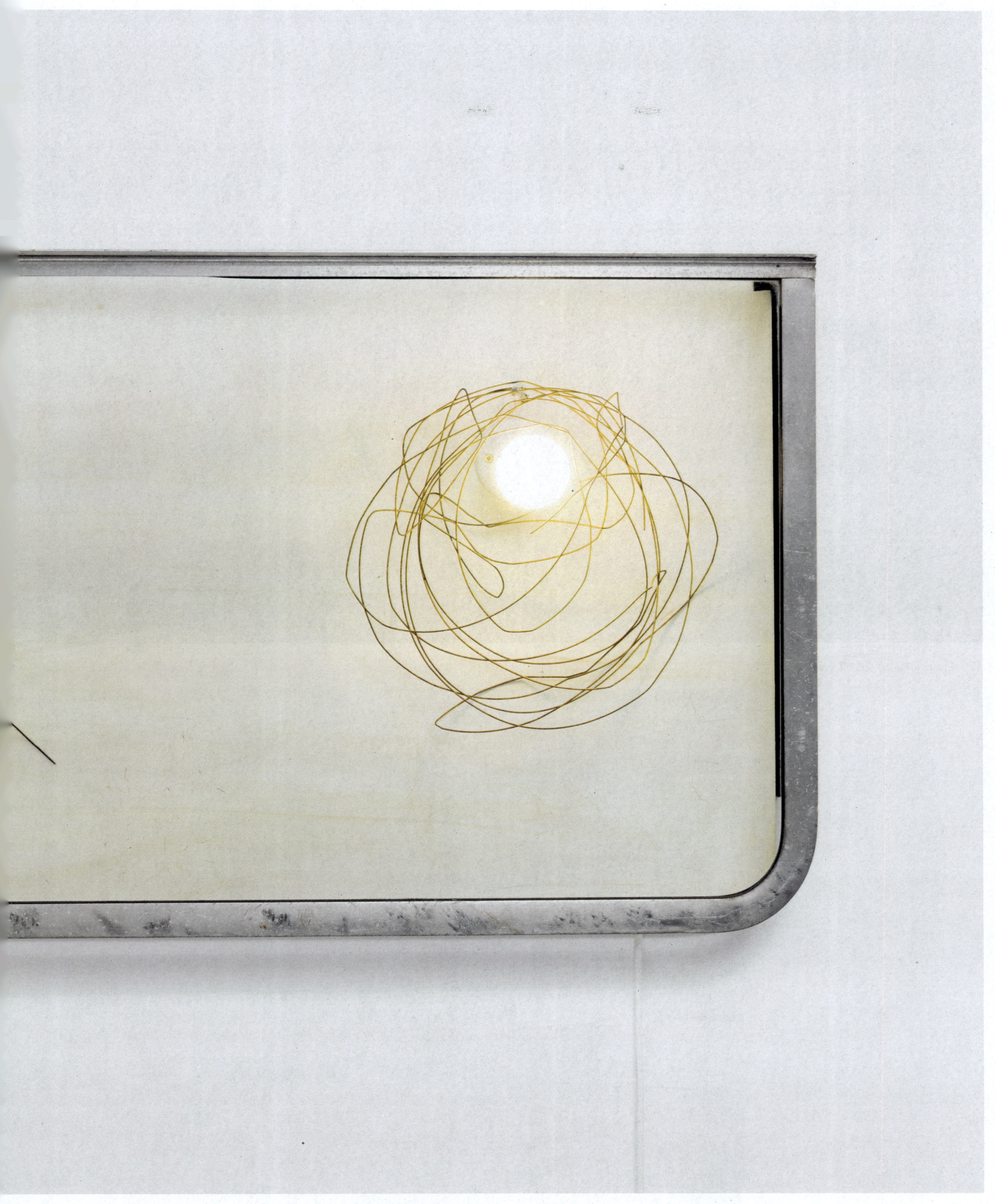

16. *Solar Tank*, **2023–2024**
**Found materials, aluminium, glass, paint, rusted wire,
rust, light, steel, copper
H 60 x W 140 x D 18 cm**

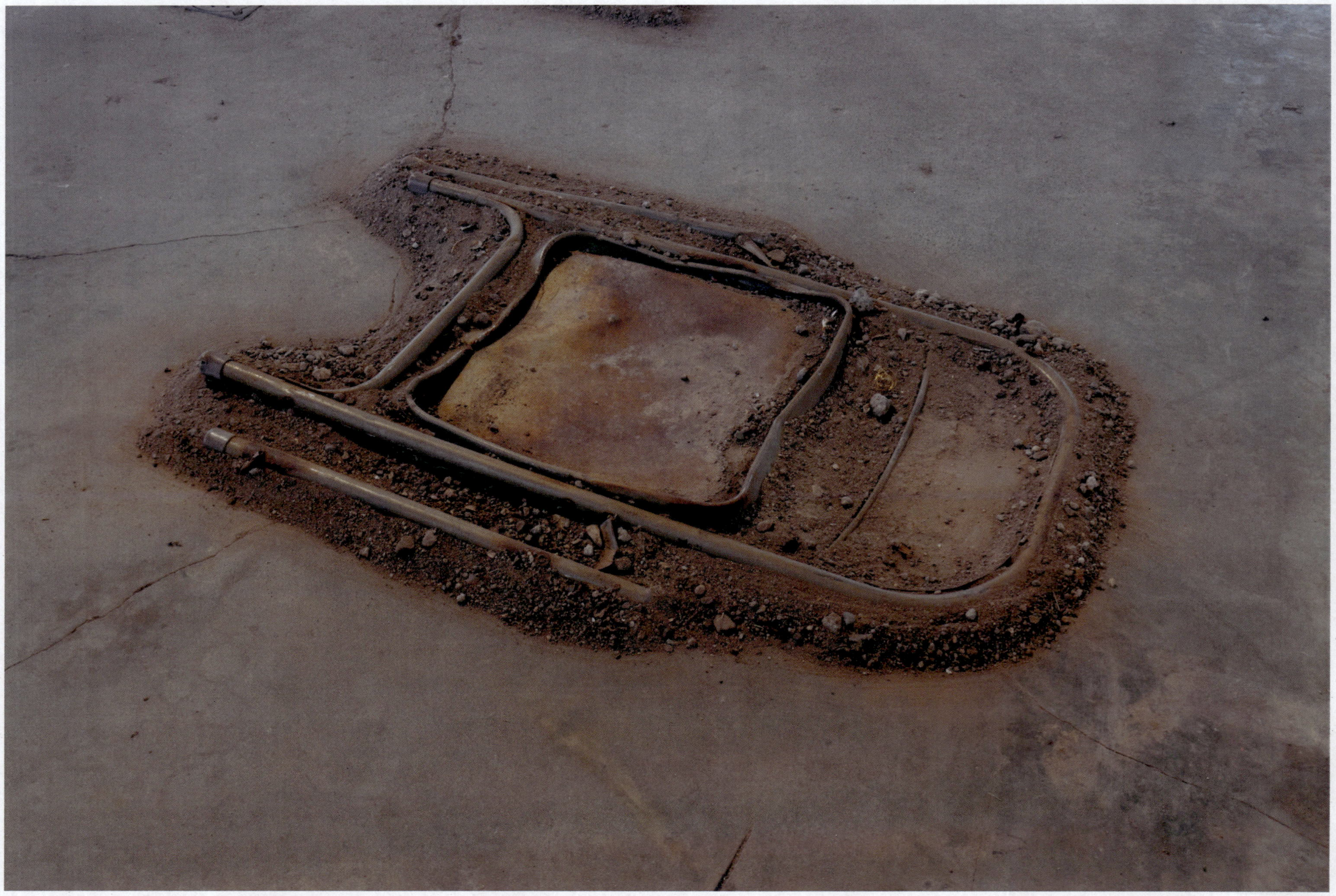

17. *Energy Field,* **2022 (detail)**

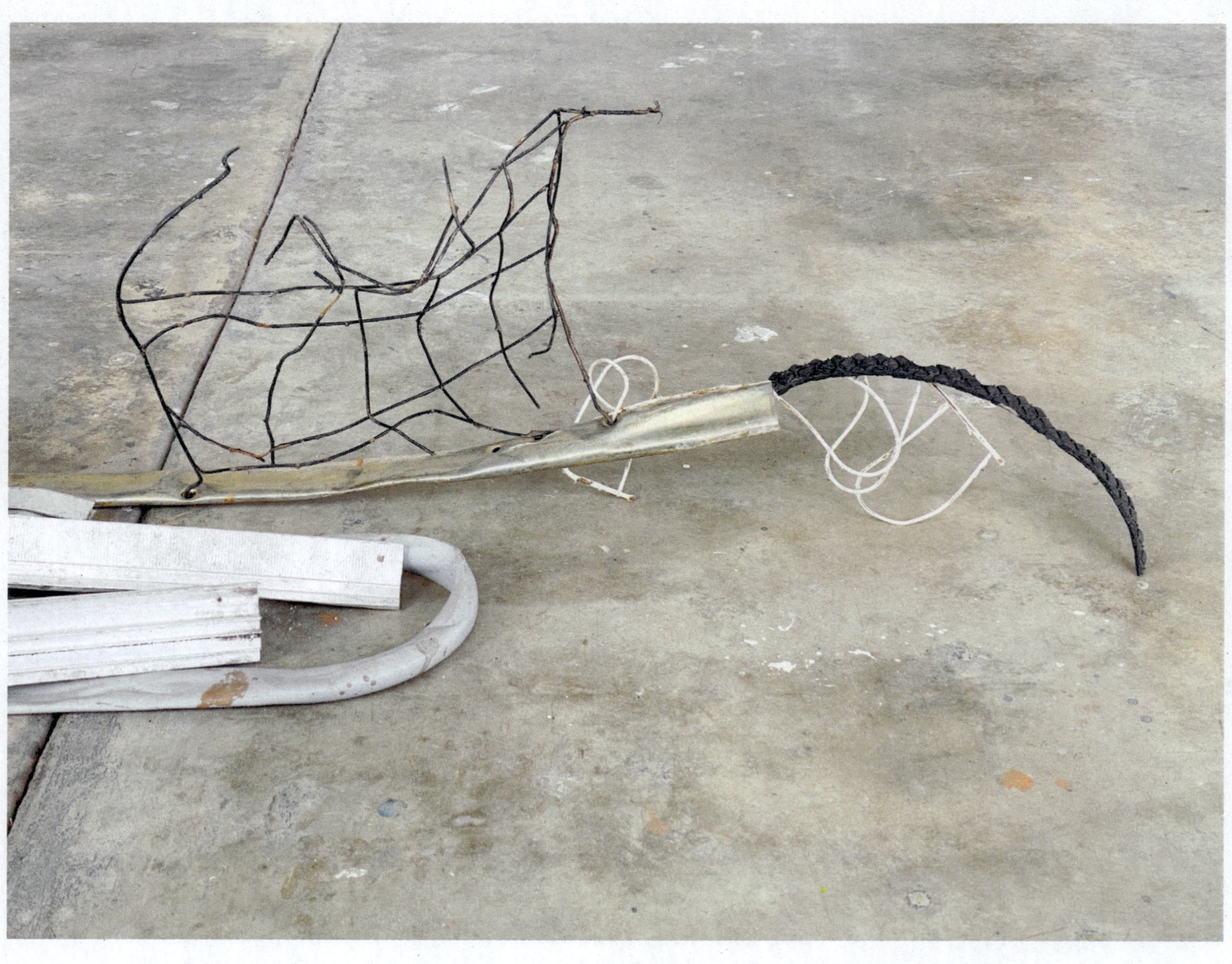

18. Accumulator (Psychic Memory), **2022–24 (detail)**

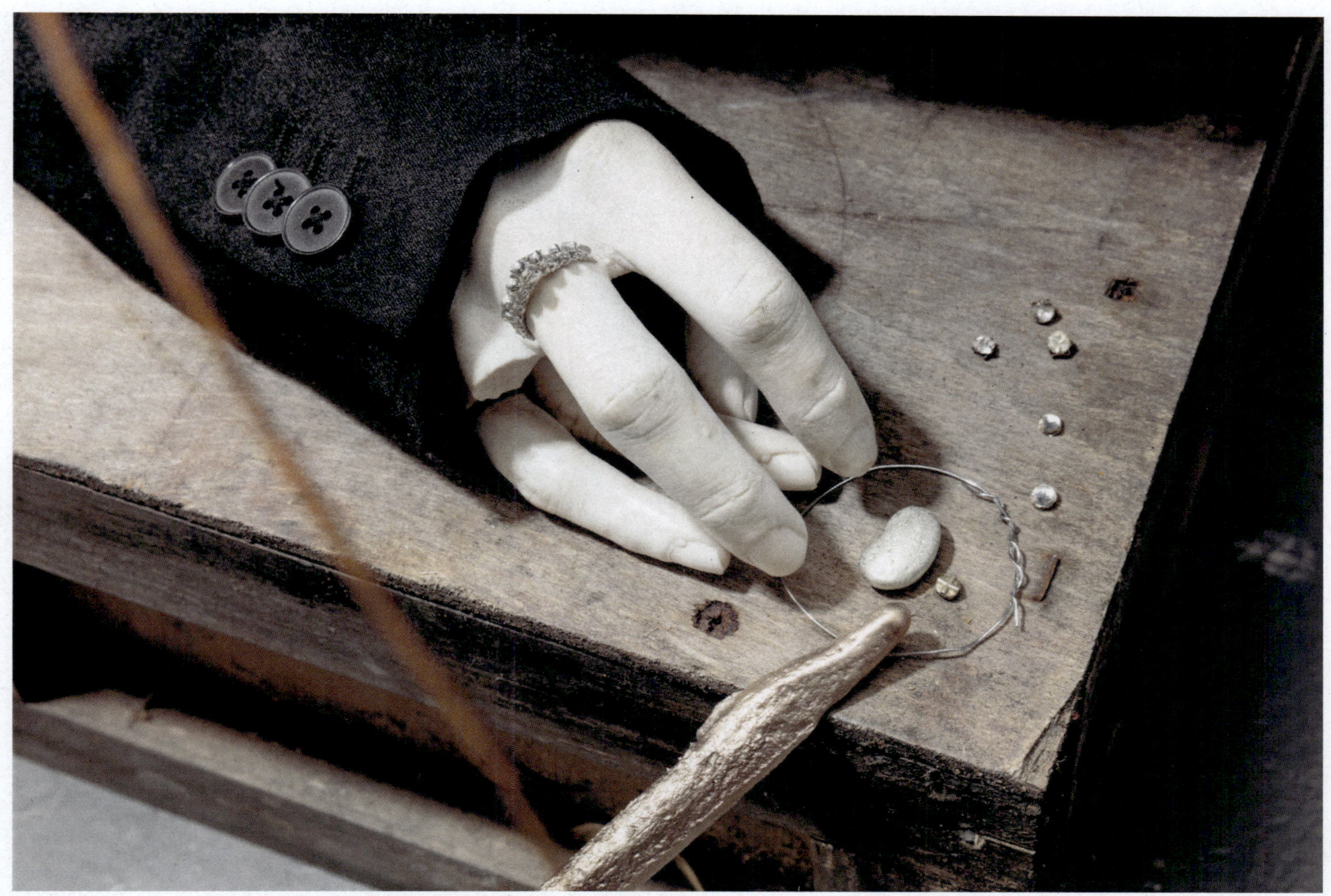

19. *Being (Immaterial),* **2023–24 (detail)**

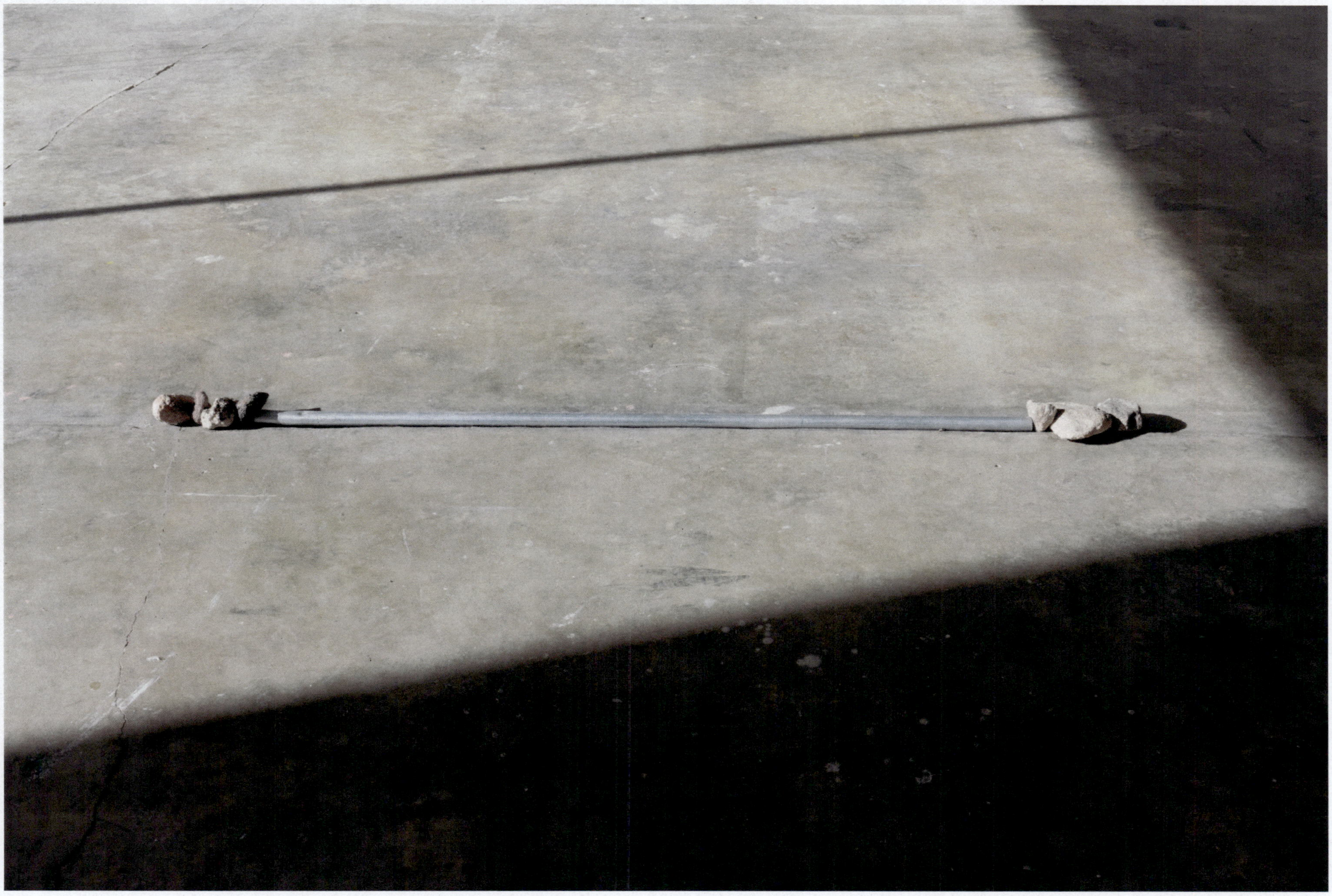

20. *Heavy Lifting,* **2022**
Found material, Chinati rocks
H 8 x W10 x L 150 cm

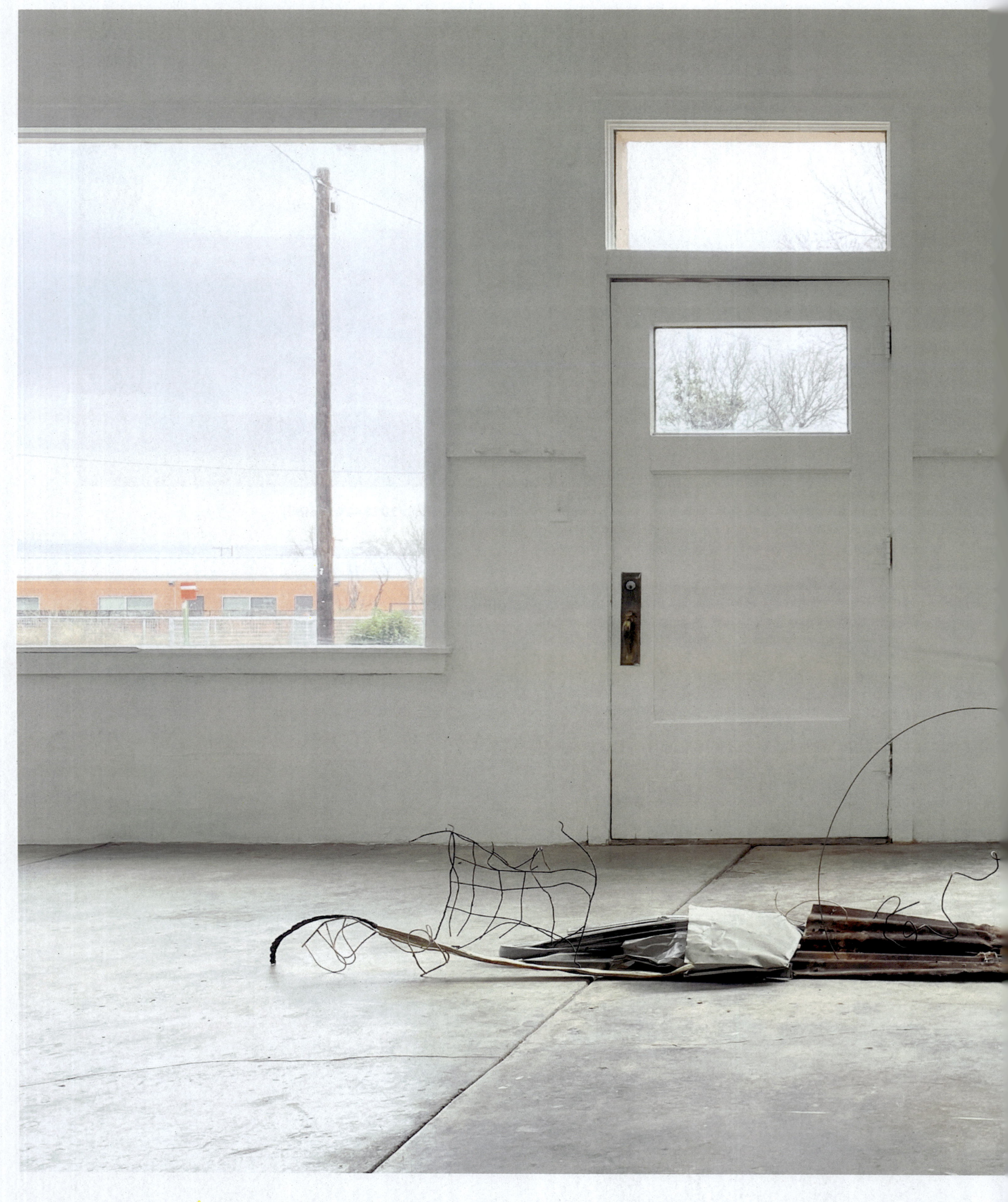

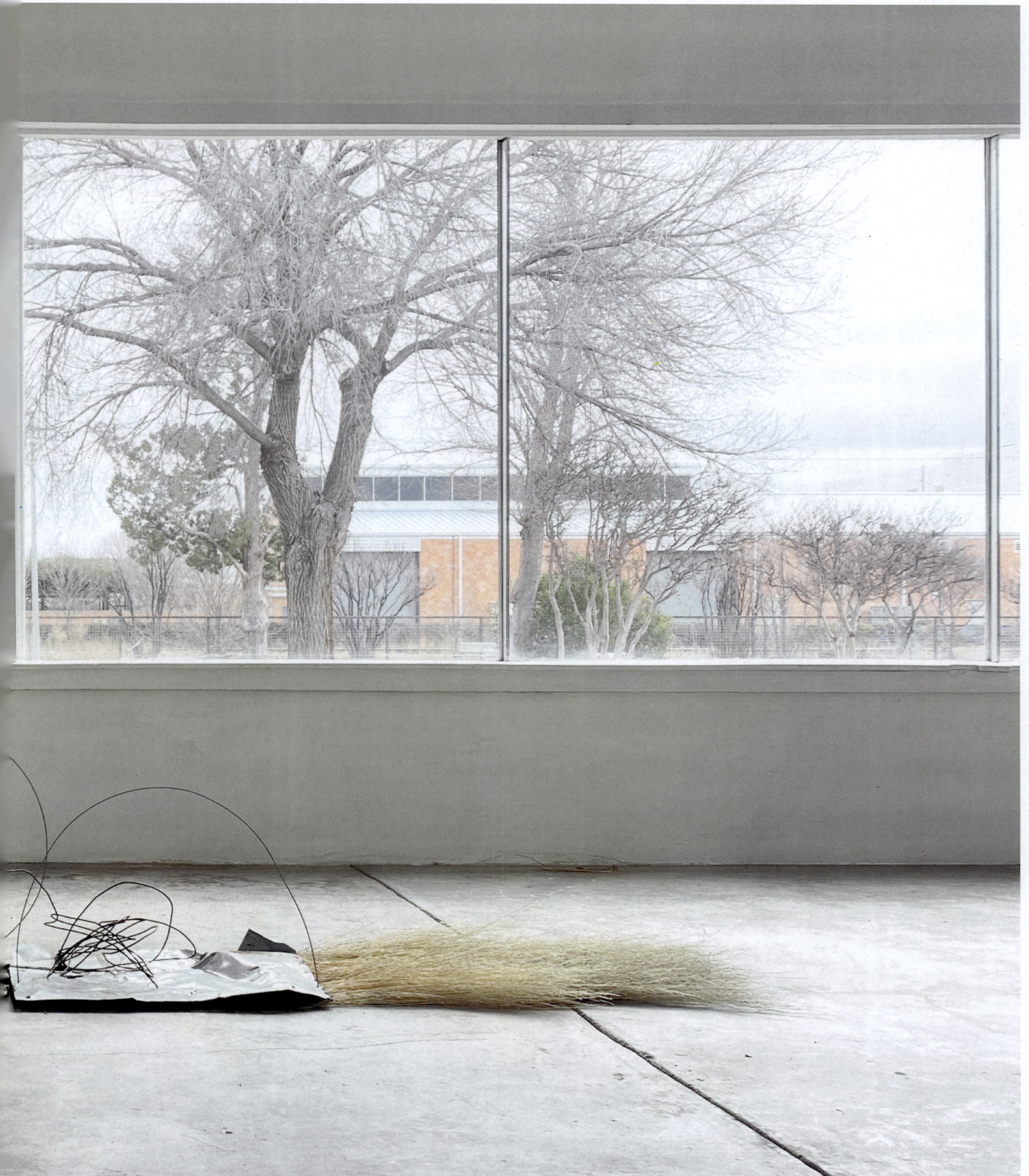

21. *Accumulator (Psychic Memory)*, **2022–24**
Found materials, Chinati grass, cast pewter
H 70 x W 51 x L 405

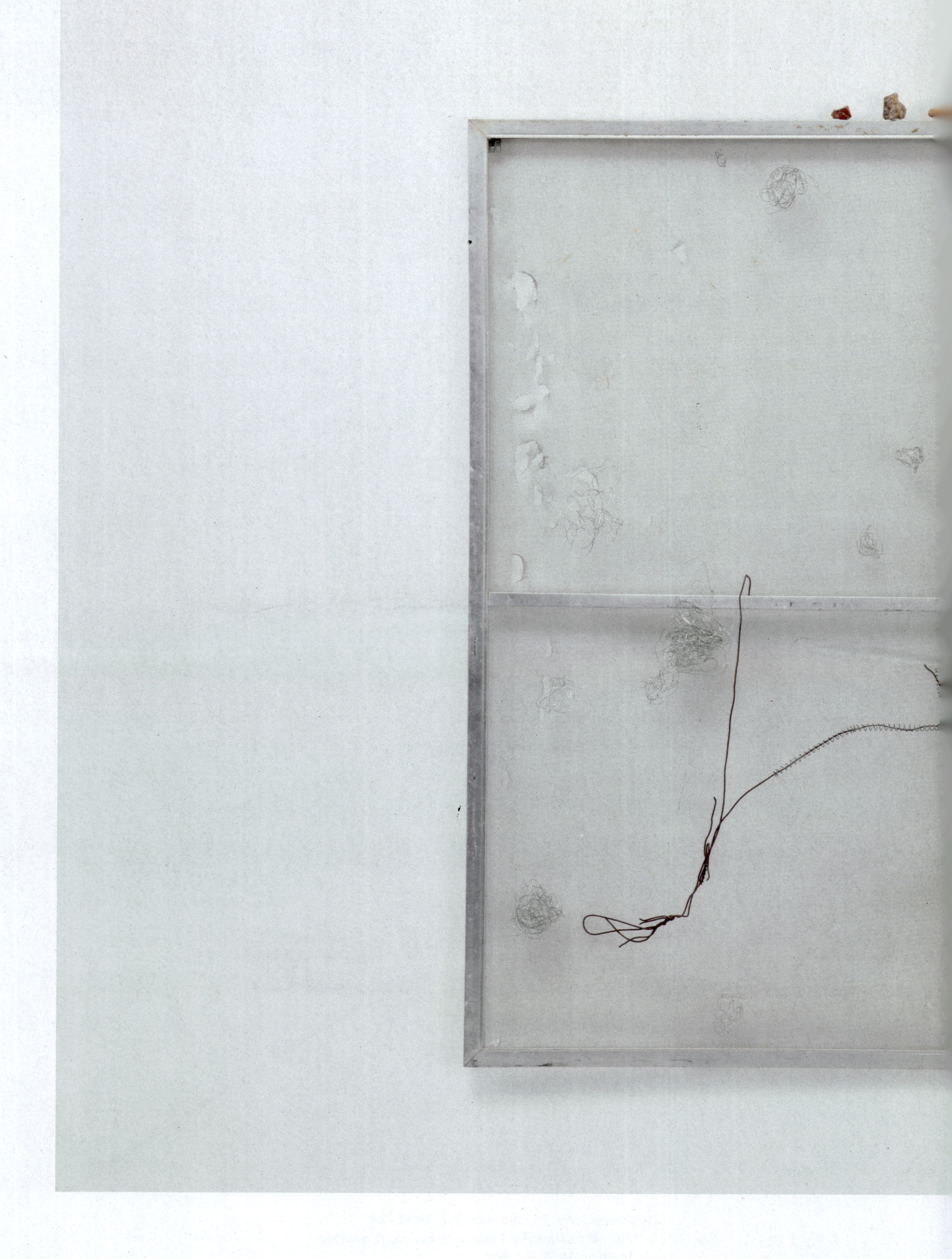

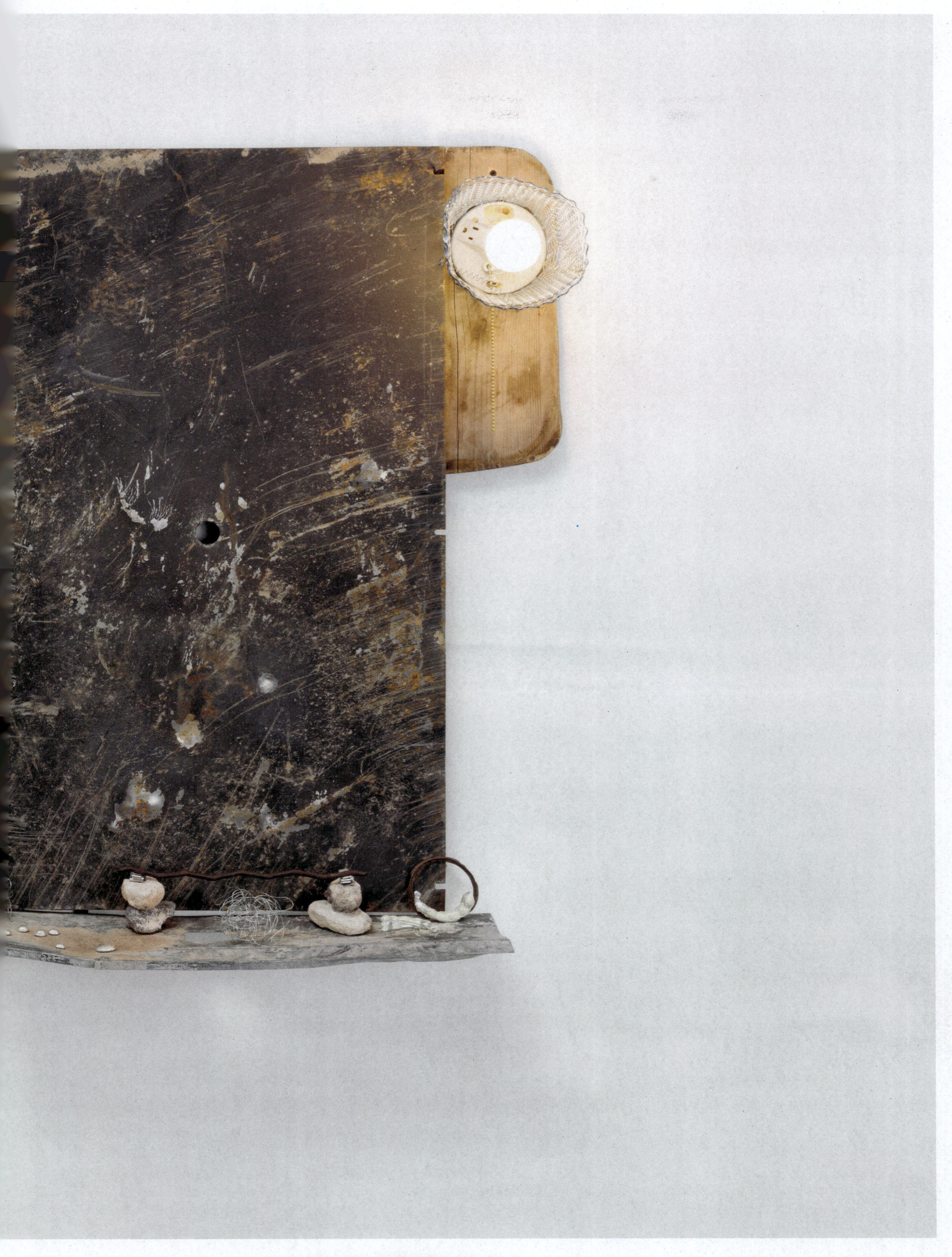

22. *Seedbed, 2022–2024*
**Found materials, wire screen, rusted steel, seeds, cast pewter,
wire, Chinati rocks, aluminium and light
H 127 x W 153 x D 25cm**

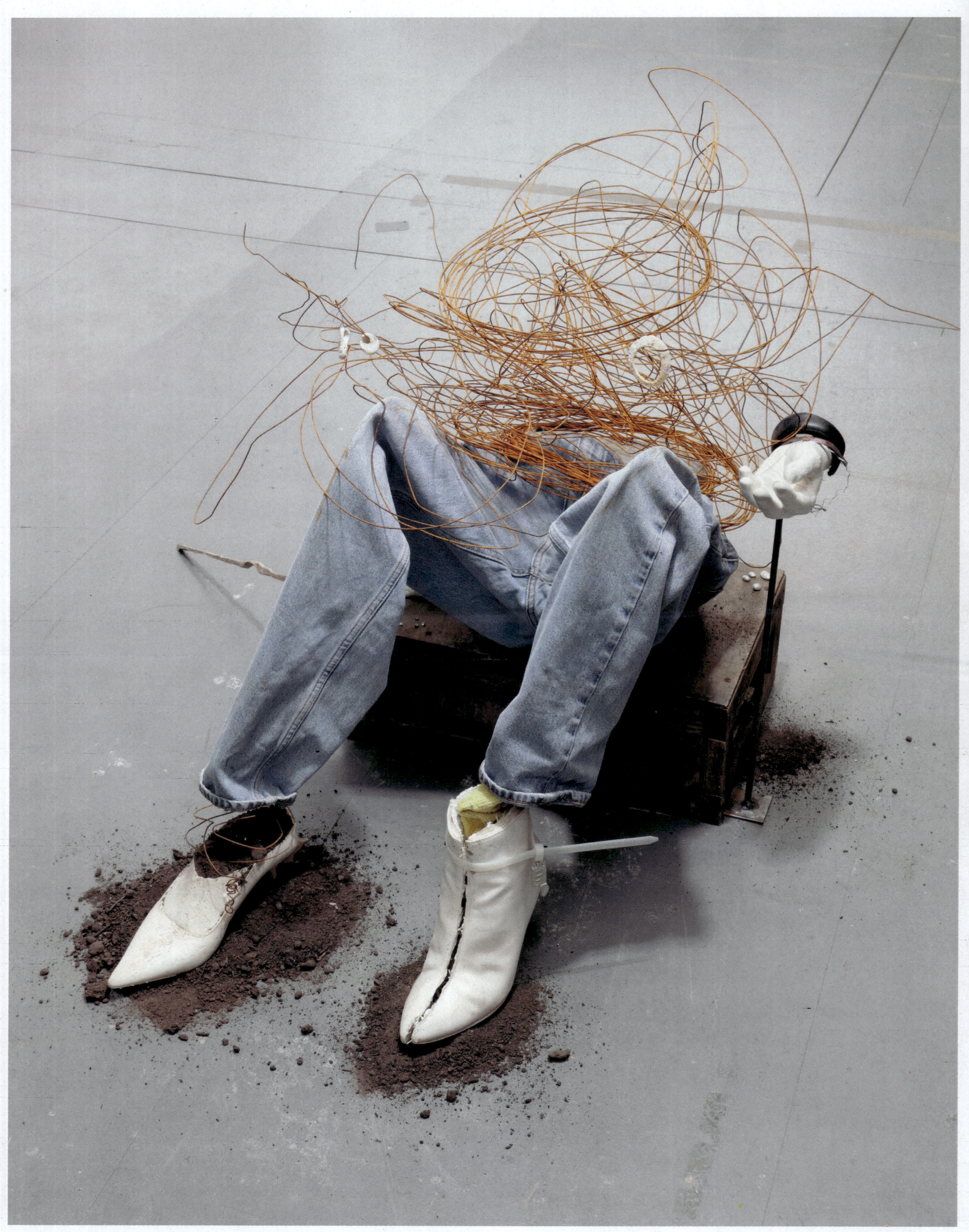

23. *Being (Immaterial)*, 2023–24
**Artists clothes, rusted wire, shells, welded steel, jesmonite, jewellery,
cast concrete, bronze, pewter, white metal, dried plant, earth
H 82 x W 116 x L 130 cm**